superstars! superstars! superstars!

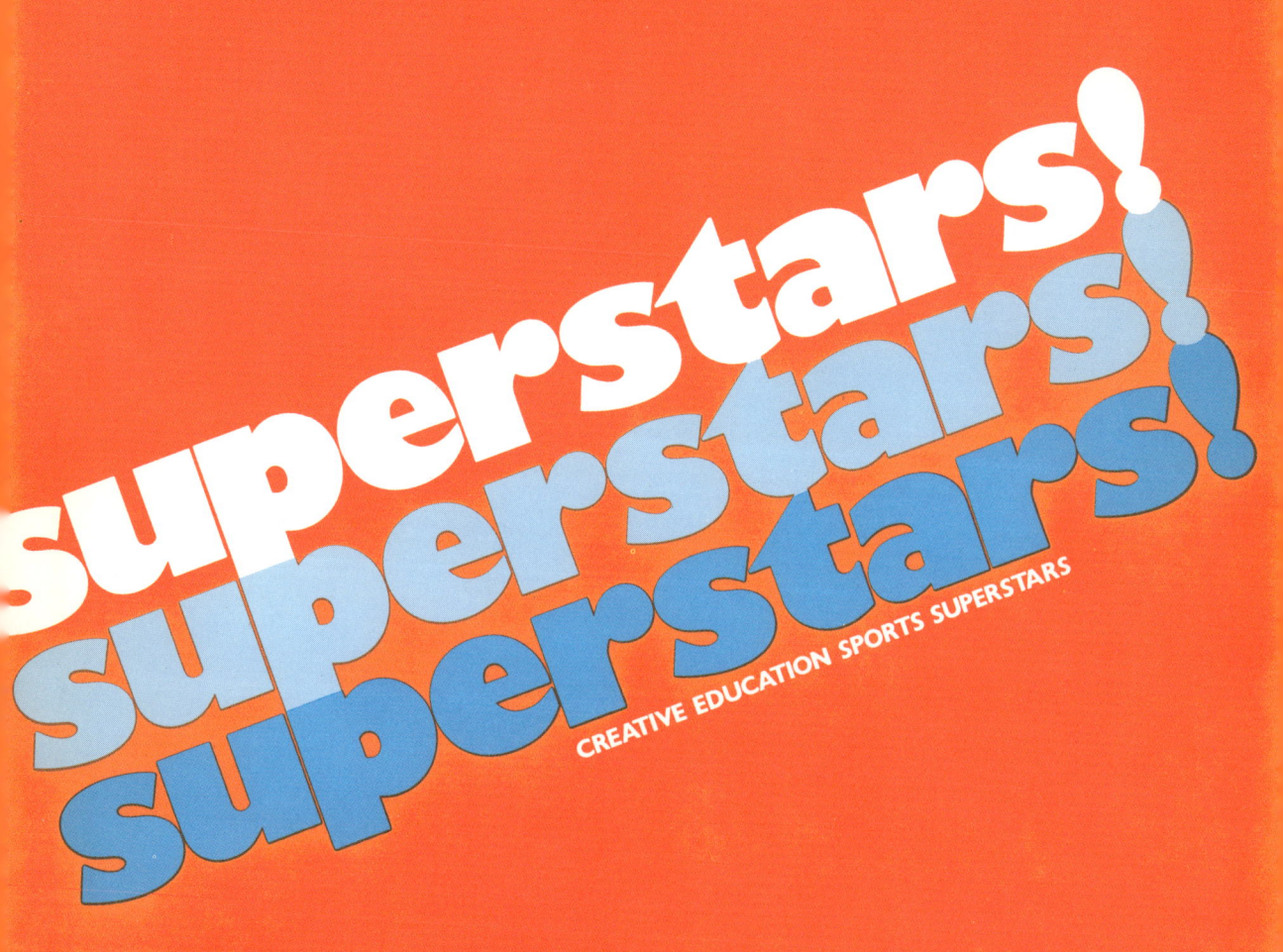

CREATIVE EDUCATION SPORTS SUPERSTARS

jackie stewart

jackie stewart

by Sam Hasegawa

illustrated by John Keely

CREATIVE EDUCATION
MANKATO, MINNESOTA

WATERLOO LOCAL SCHOOL
PRIMARY LIBRARY

796.7

Published by Creative Educational Society, Inc., 123 South Broad Street, Mankato, Minnesota 56001. Copyright © 1975 by Creative Educational Society, Inc. International copyrights reserved in all countries. No part of this book may be reproduced in any form without written permission from the publisher. Printed in the United States.

Library of Congress Number: 75-1357   ISBN: 0-87191-437-9

Library of Congress Cataloging in Publication Data
Hasegawa, Sam.   Jackie Stewart.
SUMMARY: A brief biography emphasizing the career of the race car driver who won a record twenty-seven Grand Prix races in nine years.
1. Stewart, Jackie—Juvenile literature. 2. Automobile racing—Juvenile literature.
[1. Stewart, Jackie 2. Automobile racing—Biography] I. Keely, John, ill. II. Title.
GV1032.S74H37   796.7'2'0924 [B] [92] 75-1357
ISBN 0-87191-437-9

jackie stewart
jackie stewart
jackie stewart

The roar of powerful engines washed over the track, rising and falling in waves of sound. Jackie Stewart, in the blue Tyrrell-Ford in the first row of cars, glanced at the instruments on his dashboard. It was impossible for him to hear his own engine among the 21 cars lined up on the starting grid. So he kept a careful eye on his gauges. Temperature and oil pressure were normal. The needle of the tachometer, which indicates engine speed, was at 6,500 rpm (revolutions per minute). Occasionally he pressed down hard on the accelerator, revving the engine up to 9,000 rpm.

There were only two minutes until the start of the race. It was the 1973 German Grand Prix, the eleventh round of the 15-race World Championship of Drivers competition. Jackie had already won at South Africa, Belgium, Monaco and Holland; and he was leading all other drivers in championship points.

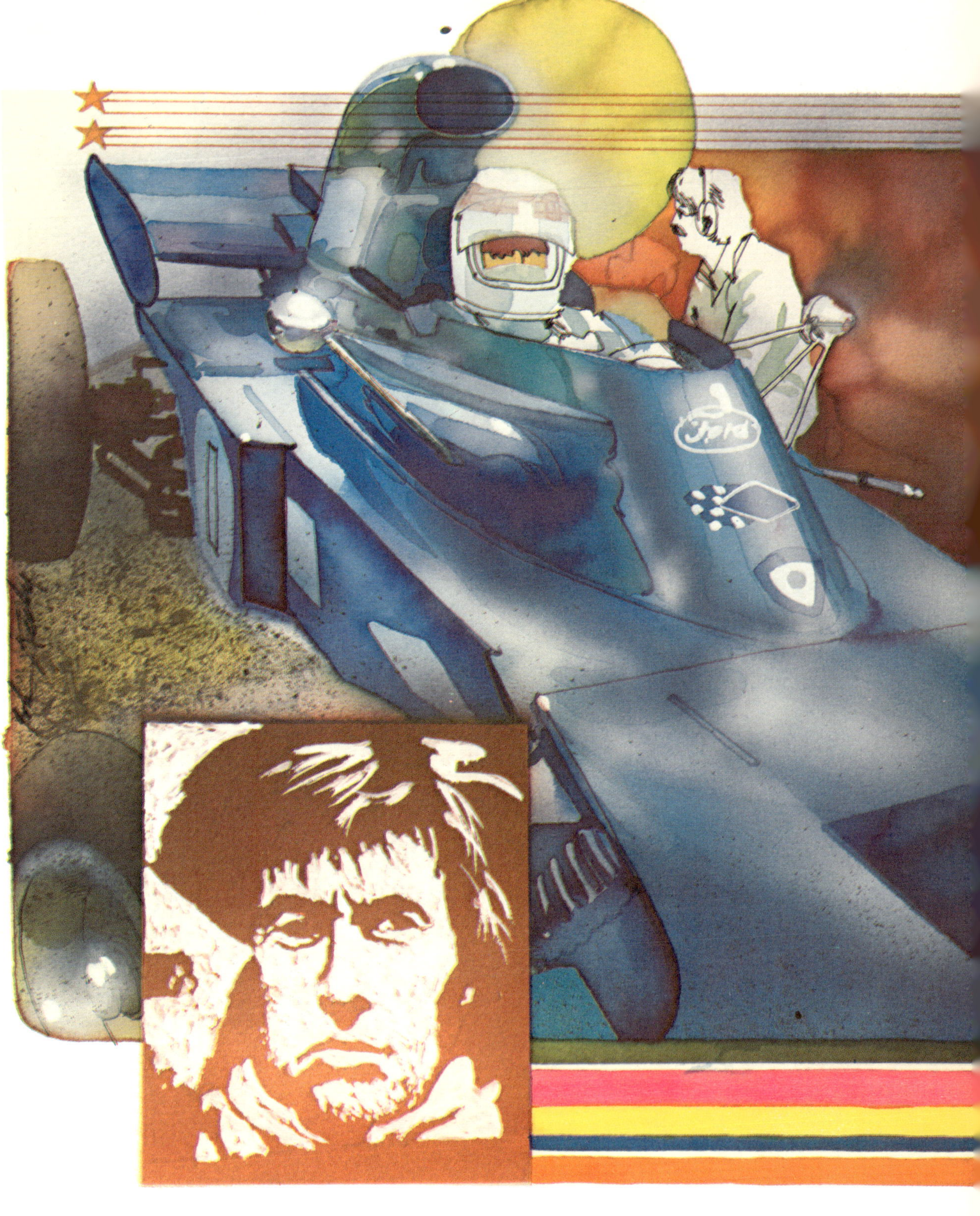

1973 German Grand Prix

But at that moment Jackie was not thinking about winning. He wasn't even thinking about racing at all. He was devoting all his concentration to staying loose and relaxed. He kept his mind free from thought, particularly thoughts about driving.

Beneath the tinted sun visor of his helmet, his face was calm and expressionless. He looked no more excited than a man waiting at a traffic signal for the light to change. Only his eyes seemed alive. His gaze shifted constantly—from the starter to the instruments on the dash to his mirrors and back to the starter again.

The man with the flag moved into position to start the race. Jackie pressed down on the gas until the tachometer needle stood at 8,500 rpm and held it there. The engine noise on the track rose to an unwavering scream.

Then suddenly the green flag flashed through the air. Jackie's Tyrrell-Ford shot across the starting line, its tires smoking. The car wriggled slightly, then accelerated straight down the road as if it were running on rails. Jackie was already well in front of the rest of the field. At the end of the straightaway he went wide to set up his line through the first turn. The car responded instantly, seeming to jump sideways across the width of the track. Then, just as quickly, it veered into the corner and disappeared from view.

There is no other road-racing course in the world quite like the Nürburgring, the site of the 1973 German Grand Prix. The track twists and turns its way through the wooded slopes of the Eifel Mountains. Over 14 miles long, the circuit contains the unbelievable total of 176 corners.

But Jackie was taking his car through the fantastic windings of the course at a tremendous speed. In less than eight minutes he had completed the first lap. Only his teammate, François Cevert, in the other Tyrrell-Ford, had managed to stay with him. When the two blue cars flashed by the grandstand, they held a seven-second lead over the rest of the field.

Jackie was in top form that day. He and his car were working perfectly together. And as always when he drove well, he felt no sensation of speed. He was always looking far down the road, anticipating the next corner. So even though he was travelling at speeds approaching 200 mph (miles per hour), Jackie did not feel as though the landscape was rushing by in a blur. Instead, it seemed as if he were watching a movie run in slow motion. Passing the grandstand, Jackie had been easily able to pick out some of his friends in the crowd.

As he took the car into the hills again, a panorama unfolded before his eyes. Forested slopes and grassy meadows; spectators sitting in the shade and standing by the corners; roadside hedges and steel safety barriers; emergency vehicles and uniformed track officials, all of these seemed to appear and then slowly disappear from the winding ribbon of black pavement.

Jackie began to make the climb up the steep hill leading to the corner called the Karussel (carousel). At 140 mph it felt like shooting upward in a high-speed elevator. Jackie had driven at the Nürburgring many times in the past. But every time he made that ascent he felt his heart pound.

The Karussel is a blind corner completely hidden from view behind the crest of the hill. Jackie aimed his car toward a tall fir tree which rose above the forest by the roadside. From experience he knew this direction would put him on the correct line through the corner.

Jackie topped the hill, and suddenly the road seemed to fall away. The car dropped down into the Karussel. The track curved into a semi-circle, banked sharply at about 30 degrees. Jackie down-shifted into second gear and gripped the steering wheel tightly.

It was like whirling around on the side of a bowl. The force of gravity pressing against car and driver was tremendous. The Tyrrell-Ford was smashed down on its suspension — its springs and shock absorbers — as far as it could go.

Coming out of the turn, Jackie felt the suspension recoil like the release of a spring. He accelerated smoothly and sped on toward the corners to come.

Driving flawlessly, Jackie continued to keep up the

Karussel a blind Corner

pace. Cevert was close behind. In tandem the two blue cars slid through the evergreen forest with clock-like precision. Their lead grew constantly greater. Eventually the rest of the field was left far behind.

Finally, after nearly 200 miles of hard driving, Jackie crossed the finish line to take the checkered flag. His winning time was 1 hour 42 minutes and 3.0 seconds — an average speed of around 120 mph. Cevert followed, 1.6 seconds behind. Nearly 40 seconds went by before another car appeared.

It had been a marvelous exhibition of driving skill. Naturally Jackie was elated. The win, his fifth of the season, gave him a huge lead in the championship standings going into the final four races of the year. And that season Jackie wanted the World Championship more than he had at any other time in his career. For 1973 was not just another year. In April, shortly after the South African Grand Prix, Jackie had made a secret decision. He had made up his mind to retire. The races of the 1973 season were to be his last.

Jackie grew up in an automotive world. His father owned a garage in Dumbarton, Scotland. Mr. Stewart's specialty was preparing high-performance sports cars for drivers who raced in local club events. And while Jackie was still in junior high school, his older brother Jimmie was making a name for himself driving in European road races.

Jackie shared the family fascination with automobiles. He quit school at 15 to work for his father as a mechanic. But unlike his brother, he was not interested in racing. At that time he was totally involved in another sport: trap shooting.

Jackie had developed a passion for shooting when he was in grade school. He spent his afternoons walking the moors around his house, a shotgun in his hand. In time he developed a keen eye, shooting at grouse and rabbits among the heather.

Later, Jackie tried his hand at shooting clay pigeons. He discovered that he was talented and became serious about the sport. By the time he was 17, he was good enough to make the Scottish national team. Shooting in international competition, he quickly became one of the best marksmen in the British Isles. By 1960 he had won the Scottish, Irish, Welsh, English and British championships.

That year it seemed certain that Jackie was headed for Tokyo and the Olympic Games. But on the day of the

Olympic trials, his twenty-first birthday, disaster struck. On one series of 25 birds, he missed eight. Jackie's dismal performance was almost unbelievable for a shooter of his talent, and it put him out of the running for the Olympic team.

He continued to shoot for several years more, but the disappointment of the Olympic trials was hard to forget. Trap shooting became less and less interesting. Eventually Jackie quit and never shot in competition again.

It wasn't long before a friend persuaded Jackie to participate in an amateur test drive at a local racing track. The two took turns driving a sports car around the course for an entire morning.

For Jackie it was an unforgettable day. He had never before driven a fast car on a track. The sensation of high-speed cornering was the finest thing he had ever experienced. After that morning he knew that he wanted to be a racer.

Jackie moved quickly from amateur to professional events. Within a few years he became well known in Scotland, driving sports cars for the Ecurie Ecosse team. By 1963 word of his performances had spread to England. Ken Tyrrell, who was then managing the Cooper Formula 3 team, became interested. Curious to see if all the reports were really true, he asked Jackie to come to England for a tryout.

Formula cars are quite different from sports cars. Somewhat like Indianapolis cars in appearance, they have open wheels and a single seat. All of them are built according to a set of rules or formula. There are restrictions on size and weight, engine design, and tire dimensions, among other things.

The different sizes of engines make the biggest difference between the various formulas. Formula 1 (F1) cars, which are used in Grand Prix racing, have 3-liter (about 183 cubic inches) engines. Formula 3 (F3) is limited to a less powerful 1.6-liter motor. Despite their relatively small engine sizes, formula cars are very fast, since their bodies are extremely light.

Jackie had never driven anything but sports cars prior to his trip to England. So before he took the Cooper F3 car onto the track, Tyrrell warned him to take it slowly at first. Formula cars are much more responsive than sports cars; so even the least bit of sloppy driving can send them spinning off the road.

Tyrrell's fear proved to be groundless. Within several laps Jackie was driving faster than Bruce McLaren, the number one driver on the Cooper F1 team. McLaren had come along to set some times for Jackie to match. Several laps later, Jackie broke the track record. Tyrrell signed him up on the spot for the 1964 Cooper F3 team.

Jackie spent only a single season in the "minor league" of Formula 3 racing. He drove in 53 races in 1964 and won 23. By the end of the year, no less than three British Formula 1 teams were trying to sign him up for the 1965 Grand Prix season.

Jackie decided to go with BRM (British Racing Motors) as the second driver behind veteran Graham Hill.

F1 cars are even more demanding than F3 cars. And the competition on the Grand Prix circuit is the toughest in the world. Each year only about 30 drivers are considered skilled enough to drive in Formula 1 races. So Jackie did not want to rush things while he was learning about Grand Prix racing. That is why he chose BRM. He knew that he would have an excellent teacher in Hill. And, as the second man on the team, he would be under no pressure to win races right away.

But if Jackie had any learning to do, he did it quickly. In the first race of the year, at South Africa, he finished sixth. He followed that up with second place finishes at Belgium, France and Holland. Then at the fast Monza circuit in Italy, Jackie shot past Hill on the last corner to win his first Grand

19

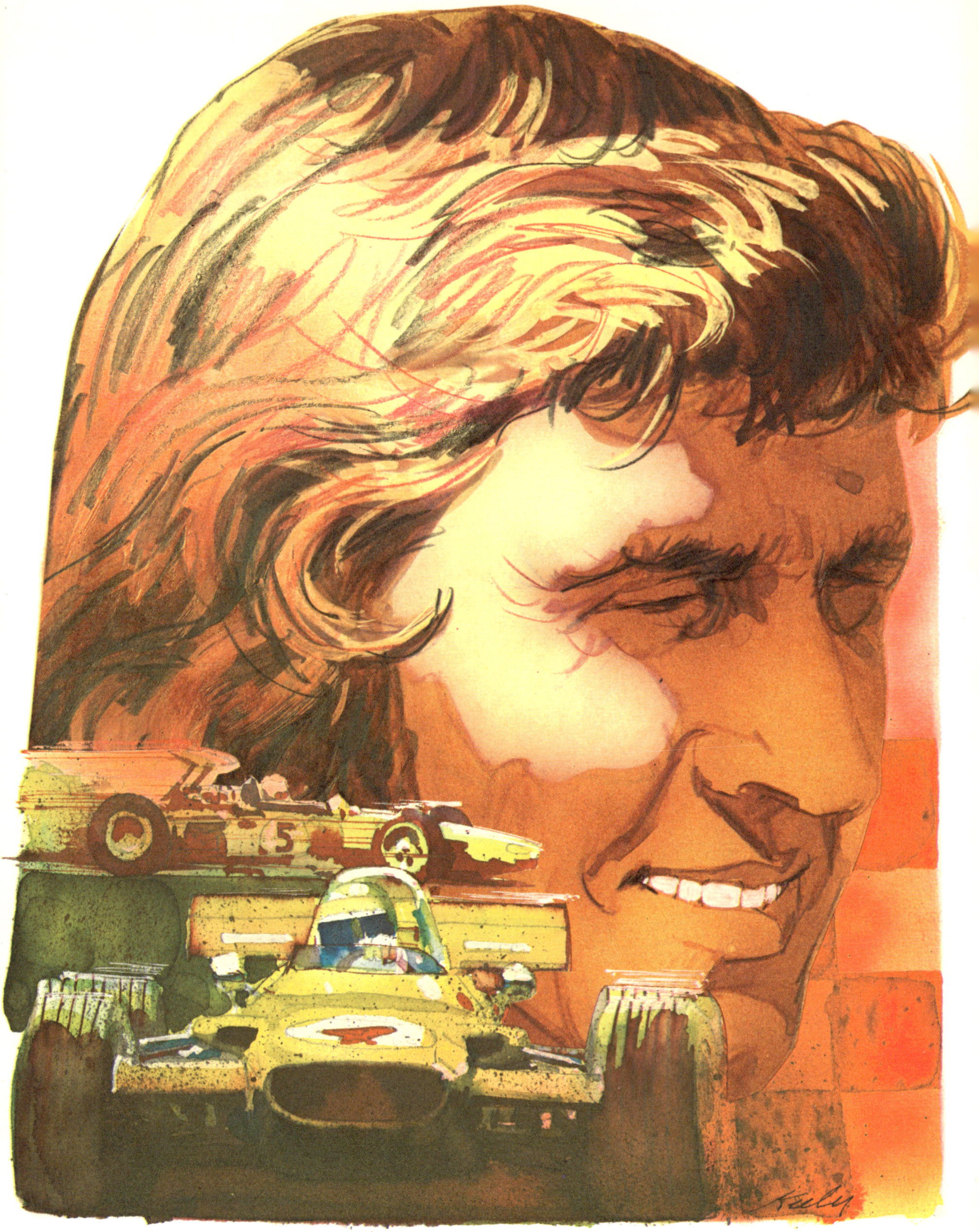

Prix. The victory guaranteed him third place in the World Championship standings. It was one of the most sensational first seasons in the history of Grand Prix racing.

Jackie had proved that he was a driver of great natural talent. But several years were to pass before he gained his first championship. Driving a car which broke down in race after race, he went through 1966 and 1967 without winning a single Grand Prix.

It was a difficult time for Jackie. But during that period he gained valuable experience. The 1966 Belgian Grand Prix, held on the circuit called the Spa, had a particularly great effect on his entire driving career.

The race began normally enough, in dry weather. But four miles from the start, near the village of Malmédy, a sudden cloudburst produced chaos. The first four cars to hit the flooded track spun off the road. Jackie, slightly behind the leaders, managed to slow his BRM enough to make it past the town safely.

But he was still travelling at nearly 150 mph when he came to an S-curve known as the Masta Kink. There the BRM flew off the slippery track, smashed through two stone fences and glanced off the side of a house. Somehow, it came to rest right side up.

Jackie was trapped in the car by the steering wheel, which was badly bent. The fuel tanks had ruptured, filling the car's cockpit with 40 gallons of gasoline. Jackie could hear the fuel pumps ticking. That meant that the electrical system was still on. And there was no way to shut it off, since the dashboard had been demolished and with it the ignition switch.

Up to his waist in gasoline, Jackie could only wait helplessly. He knew that at any second an electrical spark could turn the car into a roaring furnace. But his greatest fear was getting chemical burns from sitting in the fuel. After a period of contact, gasoline will eat away the skin just as acid does.

Jackie spent 35 minutes in the car while two other drivers searched for tools to remove the steering wheel in order to free him. Miraculously, the car never did catch on fire. But Jackie went to the hospital with a concussion, a dislocated shoulder, a broken collarbone, cracked ribs and severe gasoline burns. Eventually all his skin from the waist down came off.

Although the injuries were painful, Jackie was fortunate to have escaped with his life. But he knew that he had been lucky, extremely lucky, and he was not the type of person who liked to depend on luck. So for the first time he started to think about safety.

To prevent another situation like the Spa accident, Jackie began to drive with a wrench strapped to his steering wheel. He was the first driver on the Grand Prix circuit to use seat belts. In addition to flameproof underwear and socks, he began to wear a heavy-duty fire-resistant suit made of fiberglass. These and other precautions pioneered by Jackie have since been adopted by all drivers of F1 cars.

Jackie continued to look for ways to make racing

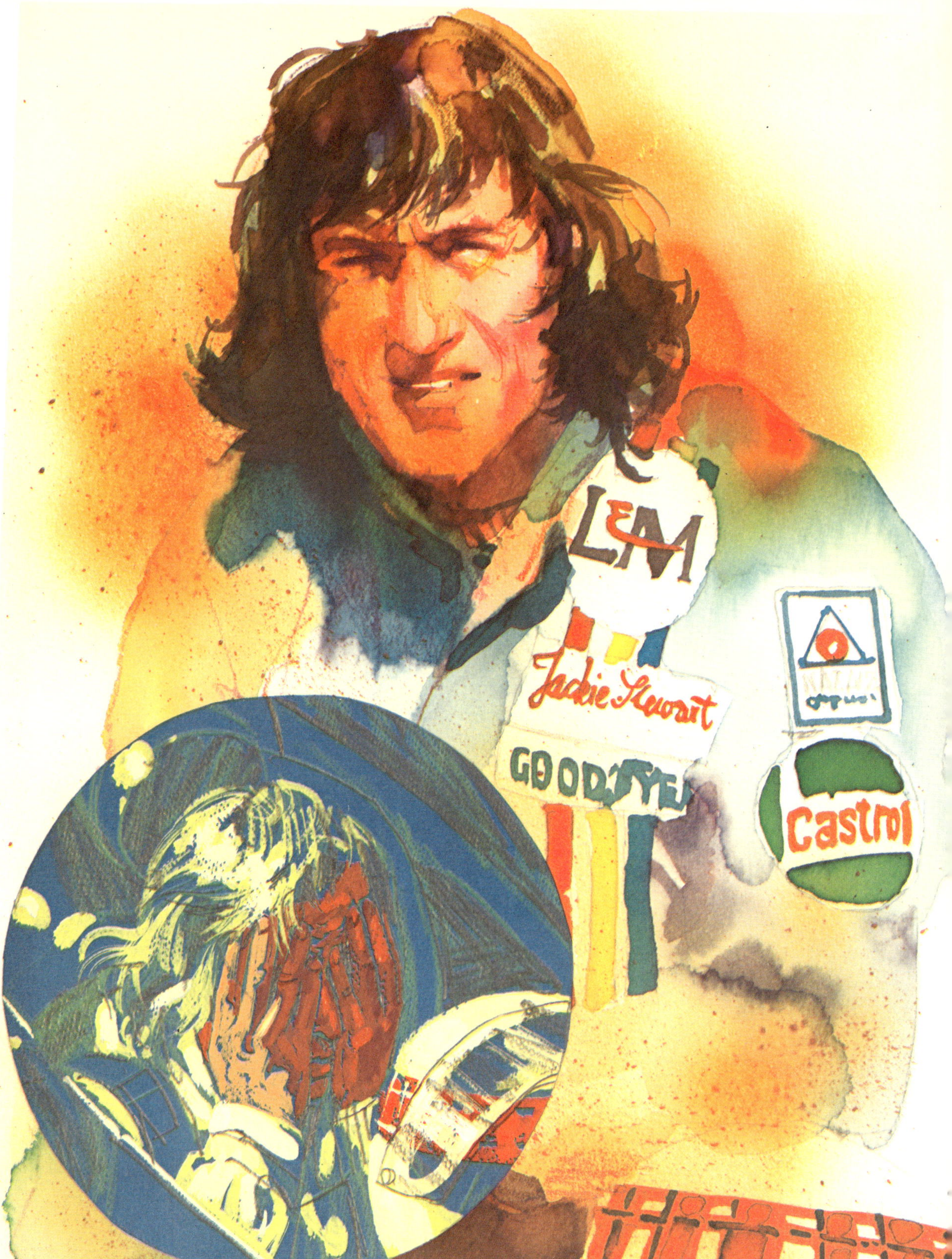

LEM
Jackie Stewart
Castrol

safer. He knew that hazards could never be completely eliminated, but he was determined to give himself the best possible odds. "You can't go through life or racing without taking some risks," he once said. "But your risks must be calculated. If you don't understand that, you are a fool."

During the 1966 and 1967 seasons Jackie gained a more professional attitude toward racing. He realized that safety was just as important as driving itself. The idea was not just to win races, but to stay alive to win another day.

Jackie's new attitude also began to affect the way he drove. From the beginning he had possessed the ability to drive fast. But as he gained more Grand Prix experience, he began to see that speed was not enough. Jackie learned that F1 cars require an extremely delicate driving touch. "The gentler you are with the brakes, the more carefully you apply the power or turn the steering," he explains, "the quicker you are likely to be." That extra bit of smoothness was what set championship drivers apart from all the others on the circuit.

Jackie left BRM in 1968 to drive a brand-new car, the Matra-Ford. Although plagued with mechanical troubles throughout the beginning of the season, the Matra proved to be far superior to the BRM. With his more polished driving style and a better car, Jackie soared into the top rank of Grand Prix drivers. He picked up three wins midway through the season and finished second in the championship.

During that season Jackie perfected a technique which made him an even better driver. He learned to control his excitement at the start of a race. He accomplished this by using a special routine. On the morning of a race, he stayed in bed later than usual. He had breakfast alone and passed the time by reading. Throughout these hours he tried to remain as calm and relaxed as possible. He tried never, even for an instant, to allow himself to think about driving.

The process continued right up to the moment the green flag came down. Feeling no excitement or nervousness, Jackie was able to make incredibly quick starts. Jumping into big leads early in the race became a Stewart trademark.

The mental discipline Jackie acquired made him an even more exceptional driver. The following year, 1969, in a new improved Matra, he was virtually unstoppable. Winning at South Africa, Spain, Holland, France, England and Italy, he swept to his first World Championship in impressive style. His season total of six Grand Prix victories was the second-best ever.

Jackie repeated the performance in 1971, driving in yet another make of car, the Tyrrell-Ford. Again he won six Grand Prix races on his way to the championship. Without a doubt, Jackie had become the finest driver on the circuit and one of the greatest of all time.

At the height of his career, Jackie lived in a constant whirl of exciting activity. His racing took him to every corner of the world. He flew over 450,000 miles yearly. Between races, there were television commentaries to do, advertisements to film and personal appearances to make.

In the time left over, Jackie managed to squeeze in

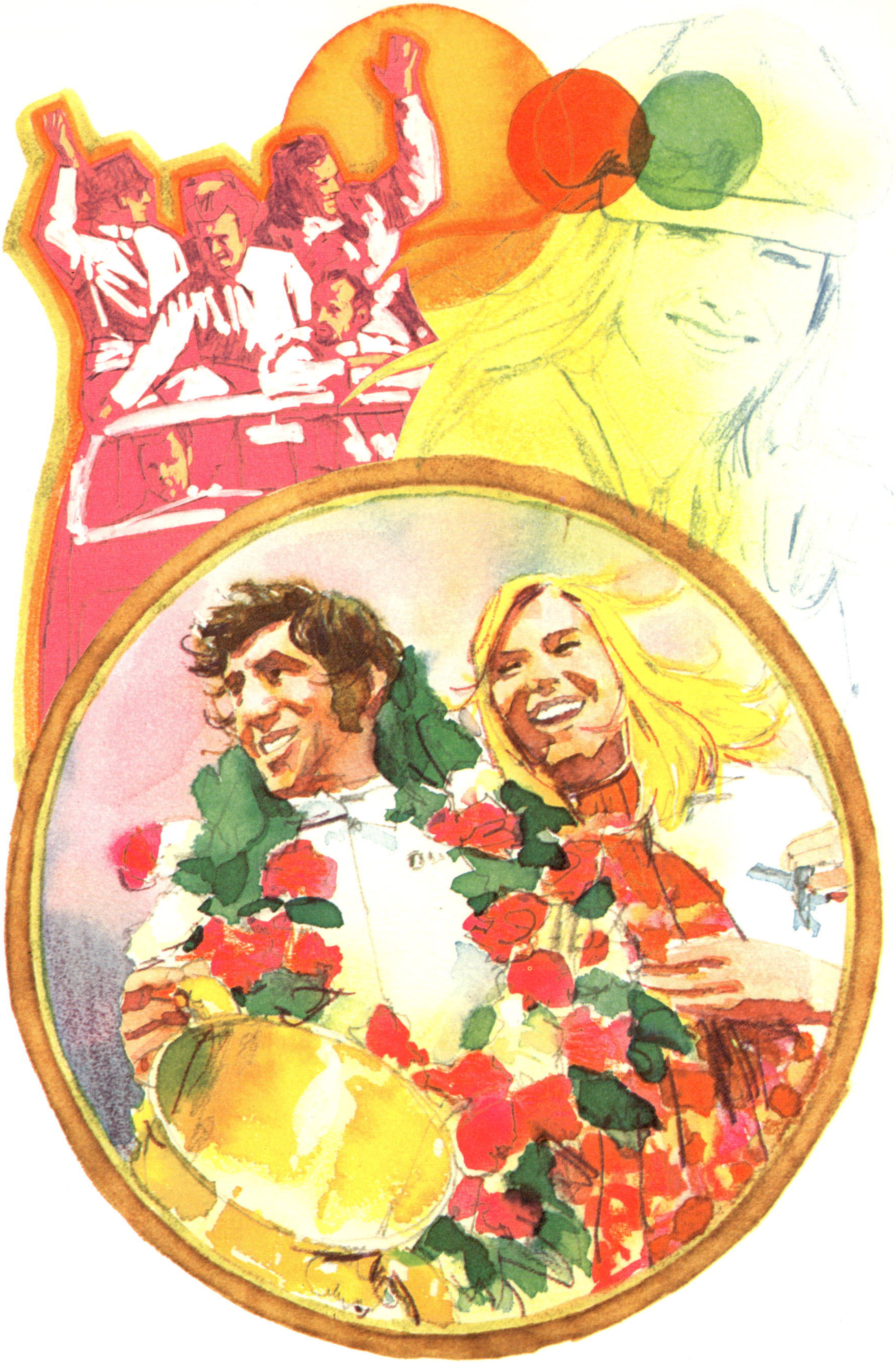

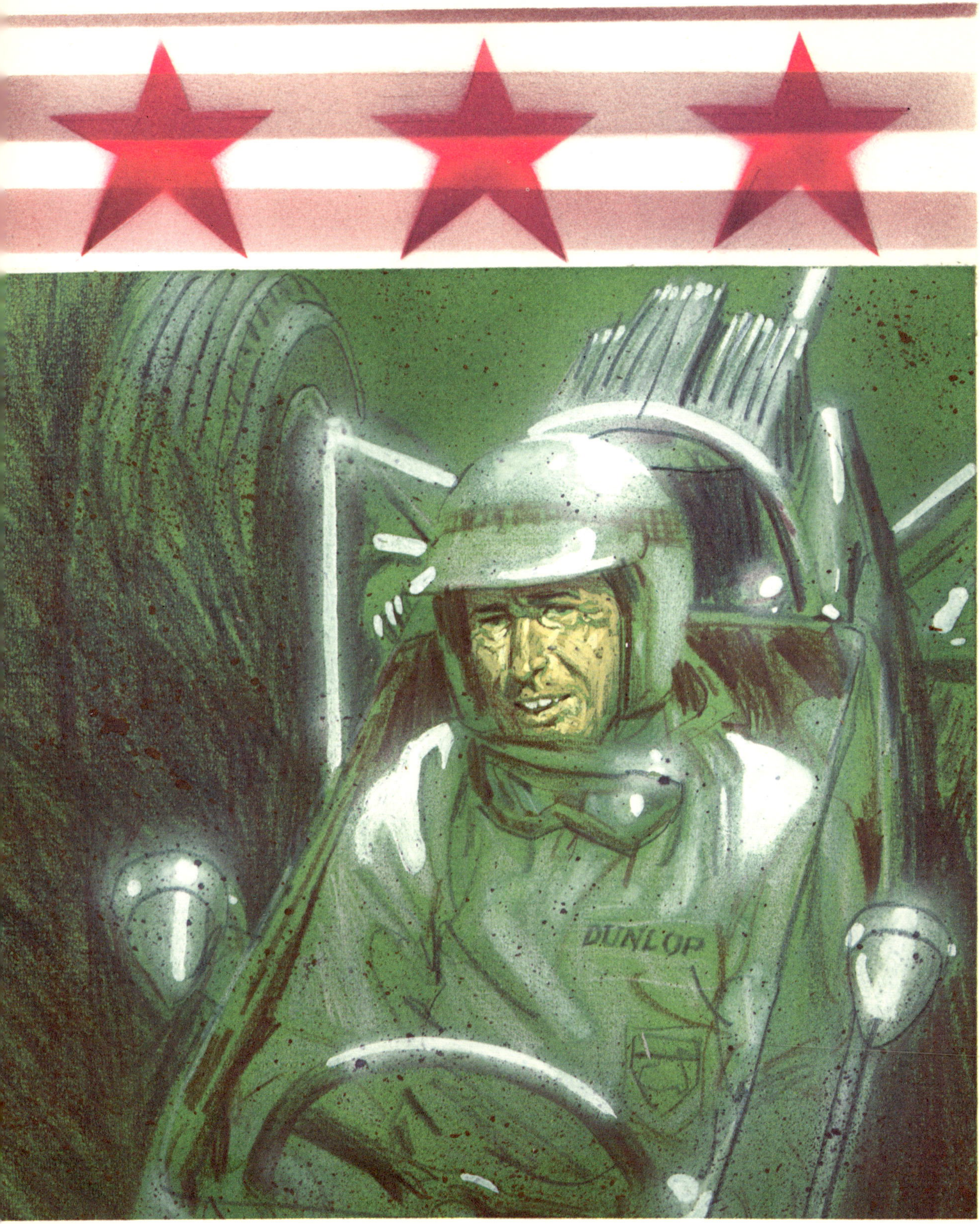
DUNLOP

a fascinating social life. Among his friends were international celebrities, nobility and the fabulously wealthy.

It was like a dream world. And it would have continued indefinitely except for one thing: death.

During his career Jackie had formed a number of close friendships with the men he drove against. One by one, each of those men had been killed in racing accidents. In 1970 alone, Jackie lost four of his best friends.

It was not that Jackie suddenly began to fear for his own life. Rather, he became intensely concerned for his wife and children. He had seen the families of his friends suffer the terrible shock and grief of a fatal crash.

Furthermore, Jackie's children were old enough to realize the risks a driver takes. The Stewarts had been living in Switzerland, in an area where there were many other racing families. Jackie's two sons went to school with children whose fathers had been killed while driving. The boys' classmates said that it was only a matter of time before Jackie, too, would be dead.

Jackie could not explain away the problem. It was impossible for him to reassure his sons. And so, early in 1973, Jackie made a decision to retire.

Jackie's victory at the Nürburgring that year turned out to be the last of his career. After that, he drove to a second-place finish at England and a fourth at Italy. Those two races gave him all the additional points he needed, and he won his third World Championship in his final year of racing.

It was a fitting ending to one of the finest motor racing careers of modern times. During nine years in Formula 1 competition, Jackie won 27 Grand Prix races — more than any other driver in the history of the sport. His career total of three World Championships had been exceeded by only one other driver. And that had been done years earlier.

But statistics tell only part of the story. Jackie did much more than just win races. He combined extraordinary driving ability with a level-headed approach to safety.

For Jackie, driving a Formula 1 car was never an act of daring. He thought of it instead as the greatest possible test of skill — requiring keen reflexes, expert hand-eye coordination and tremendous concentration. And when Jackie drove, it was clear that racing was sport in the truest sense of the word. Taking corners at the very limit of speed with incredible smoothness, he showed that driving was an art.

Football
Johnny Unitas
Bob Griese
Vince Lombardi
Joe Namath
O. J. Simpson
Fran Tarkenton
Roger Staubach
Alan Page
Larry Csonka
Don Shula
Franco Harris
Terry Bradshaw
Chuck Foreman
Ken Stabler

Baseball
Frank Robinson
Tom Seaver
Jackie Robinson
Johnny Bench
Hank Aaron
Roberto Clemente
Mickey Mantle
Rod Carew
Fred Lynn
Pete Rose

Basketball
Walt Frazier
Kareem Abdul Jabbar
Wilt Chamberlain
Jerry West
Bill Russell
Bill Walton
Bob McAdoo
Julius Erving
John Havlicek
Rick Barry
George McGinnis
Dave Cowens
Pete Maravich

superstars! superstars superstars superstars

CREATIVE EDUCATION SPORTS SUPERSTARS

Tennis
Jimmy Connors
Chris Evert
Pancho Gonzales
Evonne Goolagong
Arthur Ashe
Billie Jean King
Stan Smith

Miscellaneous
Mark Spitz
Muhammad Ali
Secretariat
Olga Korbut
Evel Knievel
Jean Claude Killy
Janet Lynn
Peggy Fleming
Pelé
Rosi Mittermaier
Sheila Young
Dorothy Hamill
Nadia Comaneci

Golf
Lee Trevino
Jack Nicklaus
Arnold Palmer
Johnny Miller
Kathy Whitworth
Laura Baugh

Hockey
Phil and Tony Esposito
Gordie Howe
Bobby Hull
Bobby Orr

Racing
Peter Revson
Jackie Stewart
A.J. Foyt
Richard Petty